Organic Beauty
Recipes

DIY Homemade Natural Body Care Products for Healthy, Radiantly Skin from Head to Toe

Make your own, facial mask, body scrubs, skin care, soap, shampoo, and balm

By

WaraWaran
Roongruangsri

"Nothing makes a woman more beautiful than the belief that she is beautiful."

- Sophia Loren

First Publish in 2015 by Pawana Publishing

Copyright © 2015 Worawaran Roongruangsri

Pawana © is a registered trademark of Pawana Publishing.

Cover and interior design by Pawana Publishing

Interior photos © Pawana Publishing

Author photo by Pawana Publishing

ISBN-13: 978-1515236368
ISBN-10: 1515236366

information herein, either directly or indirectly.

Respective authors own all copyrights not held by the publisher.

The information herein is offered for informational purposes solely, and is universal as so. The presentation of the information is without contract or any type of guarantee assurance.

The trademarks that are used are without any consent, and the publication of the trademark is without permission or backing by the trademark owner. All trademarks and brands within this book are for clarifying purposes only and are the owned by the owners themselves, not affiliated with this document.

Author's Note:

I want to thank you and congratulate you for downloading the book, *"Organic Beauty Recipes: DIY Homemade Natural Body Care Products for Healthy and Radiant Skin from Head to Toe"*.

This book contains proven steps and strategies on how to create natural and organic body and skin care products even in the comfort of your own homes and even kitchens. It has over 100 simple and easy-to-follow recipes that you can follow so you can make your own facial masks, body scrubs, soaps, shampoos and beauty balms, all using ingredients that are natural, safe and effective in helping you achieve healthy and radiant skin, from the top of your head to the tips of your toes!

If you have been relying on commercial cosmetics and drugstore products for your hair and skin care regimen, and you have been left feeling unsatisfied with the results, it is time to take matters into your own hands and make these organic body care products yourself! This e-book will let you do exactly that!

Thanks again for downloading this book, I hope you enjoy it!

WaraWaran Roongruangsri

Beauty begins the moment you decide to be yourself.

- Coco Chanel

Table of Contents

Chapter 1: Going Organic With Your Body and Skin Care

You may not realize it, but a huge chunk of your personal expenses is devoted to body and skin care products that (a) do not really work in giving you the results you want, and (b) cause you more harm than good. Shampoos, hair conditioners, skin lotions, facial scrubs, cleansers... these all tend to contain harsh and harmful ingredients. As an added insult to injury, they also cost quite a lot of money.

The introduction of more organic body care products in the market is certainly a welcome occurrence, putting our minds more at ease that we are actually putting something that do not contain the harsh chemicals that we are trying to avoid.

Unfortunately, they also happen to be even more expensive, which is the primary reason why many people are also steering clear of them. For many, they would rather make do with the 'mediocre' results that non-organic products provide instead of shelling out ridiculously high sums of money for those organic, so-called 'all-natural' products.

But there is a silver lining, and it comes in the form of you making use of your ingenuity and taking stock of the resources that you have on hand, even in your kitchen. You will be surprised at the seemingly limitless possibilities available to you.

Why Go Organic?

There are several reasons why self-proclaimed skin care experts and professionals argue against putting something that has not been 'medically tested' on your skin and body. However, there are even more reasons why you should switch from those commercial and harmful products and go organic instead.

- Organic products are safer. This is especially true for individuals who have sensitive skin and those who want to avoid having skin problems caused by harmful chemicals. Since the products are all-natural and made from the extracts of plants, there are no worries about synthetic chemicals wreaking havoc with your skin and body.

  Presently, the market is pretty much saturated with commercially produced beauty products that are chemically enhanced. The marketing strategies of the manufacturers of these products are very effective in luring consumers to buy them. Unfortunately, these products have been known to cause negative side effects, such as acne, pimples, skin rashes, discoloration, blemishes and overall dryness of the skin, to name a few. By using natural and organic products, you will be lessening the risks of exposure to these side effects.

- Organic products are proven to be the healthier alternative for your skin and body care. Not only are they safer to use, they are actually effective. Considering that they are made from some of the best and finest natural ingredients, you can count on them to improve your skin and hair quality as well as enhance your beauty.

  The benefits of organic body and skin care products are also more long lasting, especially when they are used on a regular basis.

- Using organic products is one way to contribute towards saving the environment. These days, one famous mantra is about "green living" and being eco-friendly. The chemicals often used in many skin and body care products have been identified as detrimental to the environment. They have also been found out to be the cause of many diseases and health problems.

- You may have difficulty believing this at first, but organic products will actually save you money in the long run. Granted, many products that are labeled as 'organic' come with expensive price tags. But, in the long run, you will obtain more savings with organic products.

This is a scenario that has played countless times before for many individuals. A young woman chooses to buy a commercial beauty product and uses it on her face, thinking that it is much cheaper than one with an organic label. Not long after applying the product on her face, the harsh chemicals cause her skin to break out and red marks to appear. In a worst case scenario, scars and pimple marks will develop. She will then have to consult with a dermatologist and undergo a series of skin treatments in order to clear her face of the breakouts and get rid of the scars.

Now those treatments do not come cheap, and the products that will be prescribed to solve the problem are also likely to be expensive. In the end, she will end up spending more.

- Making your own organic beauty products also provides assurance that no animals are harmed in their formulation. Advocates of animal welfare are always going on and on about how some manufacturers' practices are unethical, including laboratory and animal testing.

In this context, is "organic" the same as "natural"?

Many are under the assumption that an organic product is automatically natural. Well, not completely.

Natural body and skin care products are those that are formulated using ingredients from natural sources, such as plants. However, the method of cultivating these natural sources may not coincide with what is considered to be sustainable farming practices.

This is where the distinction comes in. Organic ingredients, which make up the organic beauty products that are included in this e-book, are:

(1) cultivated through sustainable farming practices; and

(2) cultivated without the use of chemicals, such as pesticides, herbicides and insecticides.

A beauty product may be natural, but not organic. However, organic products are natural.

Take, for example, a body scrub with honey as its main ingredient. It is natural, since it is made from honey, but that does not necessarily mean it is organic. For it to be categorized as an organic body care product, the honey used must have been cultivated through sustainable farming practices.

Here's a great piece of news to those who want to switch to organic products. In the past, there was a bit of difficulty getting your hands on these products, but as the demand for organic beauty products is rising, more and more retailers are now selling them.

Chapter 2: Do-It-Yourself Organic Products

We all appreciate the convenience of going to the nearest store and simply taking our pick from the rows and rows of organic beauty care products available. But here is one option that most have thought of but did not really pursue: DIY or do-it-yourself organic beauty care products.

And so we come to the next question: why should you make them yourself? Why DIY products for the treatment of your skin, hair and body?

DIY beauty products are guaranteed to contain safe ingredients.

There is one huge advantage of using homemade body products that you have made yourself: the assurance that they are safe. Naturally, as you followed the recipes and made your own facial scrub, body wash, or even shampoo, you will make use of only the safest ingredients. Thus, you can rest assured that what you are putting on your body are truly 100% organic and natural.

What about those commercially produced organic products that are filling up those long shelves in the supermarket and even drug stores?

There is no assurance that the list of ingredients appearing on the product labels is followed. In fact, there is a great chance that the manufacturers of these products are adding ingredients - especially those that prolong their shelf lives - without indicating them on the labels. In short, these products do not really conform with what is stated on their respective labels. More often than not, only a certain percentage of the ingredients are organic; the rest are not.

What many consumers are not aware of is that manufacturers usually add unnecessary ingredients to their products. In fact, most of the more expensive brands add a lot of water. Making it yourself will guarantee that you will only be putting beneficial ingredients - those that are actually effective - in your beauty treatment product.

Many organic products that are commercially manufactured and marketed have been found to be only partially organic. True, their main components may be organic, but the rest are not. With homemade products, you can be sure that the treatment you are using is 100% organic.

Homemade products can be customized according to the user.

If you make your own facial creams, masks and lotion, you are the one in charge. You can choose which ingredients to add, customizing the product to your own preference. If you do not prefer strong scents, you can choose mild-scented ingredients instead.

Let us say, for example, that you have a particularly sensitive skin, especially on your face. You have tried many different types of products but none of them work. Worse, they even aggravate the problem and cause your skin to break out even more.

By making your own facial scrubs and facial masks, you can choose the ingredients that are especially effective in caring for sensitive skin, and steer clear of those that do not really do much.

The possibilities are endless once you set your mind to creating your own organic beauty products. You can get ingredients from various sources, such as fruits, vegetables, herbs, nuts and even grains. There are also animal-based products that you can incorporate into your recipes, such as honey and egg.

DIY products are much cheaper.

Another advantage of going DIY with your beauty products is the cost. You will be surprised at how much mark-up is placed on the cost of the beauty products that are being sold by established manufacturers, especially those that are marketed as organic.

A large reason why these commercial products are so expensive is the chemical content added to them. Since you are doing away with those chemicals when you make your own treatments at home, you will be able to save money.

There is one important thing that everyone must do before launching into making their own line of homemade beauty products, though: research.

Learn about the state of your skin and hair and find out what you need in order to address the issues that you are currently having. You should also do some research on the ingredients that you are thinking of using, and make sure that you avail them from organic sources.

Chapter 3: Homemade Organic Products for the Face

The face is deemed by many as the part of the body that needs a lot of care. In fact, people tend to spend more money on facial products more than other types of beauty products. Since facial skin is sensitive, more care and caution are practiced when it comes to choosing what will be applied or used on it. Here are some of the easy to follow recipes of effective homemade organic facial treatment products.

I. **Aloe-Papaya Facial Mask**

Name one ingredient often used in beauty products and papaya would be immediately mentioned. Aloe vera, on the other hand, is known for its many healing properties, which makes is a favorite herbal ingredient in various applications.

Ingredients:

1/4 pc ripe papaya, sliced or diced

2 tbsp aloe vera gel

2 tbsp green cosmetic clay

Procedure:

Combine all ingredients and puree them until a thick paste is formed.

Application:

1. Spread the paste all over your face and neck, massaging gently.

2. Leave it on for 15 to 20 minutes.

3. Rinse off the paste with lukewarm water.

II. **Artichoke Facial Mask**

Artichoke may not be one of the first things that will come to mind when it comes to homemade beauty products, but it actually has properties that aid in cleansing your skin and keeping it moisturized.

Ingredients:

1 pc fresh artichoke heart (or canned artichoke hearts in water)

1 tsp lemon juice (lemon extract) or vinegar

2 tsp olive oil (canola oil or avocado oil will also work)

Procedures:

1. If using fresh artichoke hearts, cook it first until soft. If using canned artichoke hearts, make sure they are canned in water and not in oil.

2. When cooled, mash the artichoke hearts.

3. Mix oil and lemon juice (or vinegar) with the mashed artichokes.

4. Stir vigorously until a smooth paste forms.

Application:

1. Massage the paste on the face and neck, using circular motions.

2. Leave the paste as a mask for 10 to 15 minutes.

3. Rinse off the mask with warm water.

III.   **Almond-and-Honey Facial Scrub**

The key to this recipe is to ensure that the almonds are crushed finely so they can act effectively as a facial scrub.

Ingredients:

2 tbsp almonds, crushed or ground finely

1 tbsp honey

Procedures:

Mix ingredients together.

Application:

1. Apply on face and neck, scrubbing and massaging gently using upward, circular motions.

2. Leave it on for 3 to 5 minutes, and rinse with warm water.

IV.   **Avocado Facial Mask**

Avocado is known to have hydrating properties, making it ideal for dry skin.

Ingredients:

½ pc ripe avocado, sliced or cubed

1 tsp vegetable oil (olive oil is another option)

Procedures:

1. Slice or cut avocado flesh for easier mashing.

2. Mash the avocado, mixing in the oil.

3. Mash and stir until a thick paste is formed.

Application:

14

1. Apply the paste as a facial mask.

2. Leave the mask on for 10 to 20 minutes, depending on degree of skin dryness.

3. Rinse off paste with warm water.

V. **Avocado-Banana Facial Mask**

Those who are suffering from dry skin that is also sensitive will find a friend in this avocado-banana combination.

Ingredients:

½ pc ripe avocado, sliced or cut

½ pc ripe banana, sliced or cut

2 tbsp plain yogurt

1 tsp wheat germ oil

Procedures:

1. Mix the sliced avocado and banana in one bowl and mash them together.

2. Add the plain yogurt and wheat germ oil and stir until it turns into a paste.

Application:

1. Apply paste to clean and dry face and leave it on for 10 to 15 minutes.

2. Rinse off paste with warm water.

VI. **Banana Facial Mask**

Sensitive skin will benefit from this facial mask which makes use of banana as its primary ingredient. It works well as a moisturizer, thanks to its soothing effect.

Ingredients:

1 pc ripe banana, sliced or cut

1   tsp vinegar

Procedure:

Mash the banana until it becomes a paste.

Application:

1. Apply banana paste on the face and leave it on for 10 to 15 minutes.

2. Mix vinegar with warm water and rinse off the paste.

VII.   **Carrot Facial Mask**

People with oily skin may turn to carrot as their lifesaver. Carrot also has properties that are good for clearing acne, blemishes, and pimple marks.

Ingredients:

2 pcs large carrot (or 3 pcs small- to medium-sized carrots)

1 tsp lemon juice or lemon extract

1 tsp apple cider vinegar

5 tbsp honey or plain yogurt (optional)

Procedures:

A. Uncooked carrot facial mask

   1. Grate the raw carrots, but make sure the juice remains with the grated portion. Do not drain.

   2. Add lemon juice, and mix until they are well-blended.

B. Cooked carrot facial mask

   1. Boil the carrots until soft.

   2. Mash the boiled carrots (you may also use a blender or a food processor).

   3. Add lemon juice and honey or yogurt. Stir until well-blended.

Application:

1. Massage the mixture on your face using upward, circular motion, and spread it, paying extra attention to the oiliest parts. It would be best to do this lying down so they will not fall off.

2. Leave on for 15 to 20 minutes.

3. Rinse with warm water mixed with vinegar, using it as a final rinse.

VIII. **Cucumber Facial Mask**

Cucumber happens to be one of the most popular ingredients for facial treatments, so why not turn it into a facial mask for maximum effect?

Ingredients:

½ pc cucumber

1 egg, with egg white separated from yolk

1 tbsp lemon juice or lemon extract

1 tsp mint extract or 1/2 cup mint leaves (minced)

Procedures:

1. Mix all ingredients. Blend or puree until it develops into a paste. Use only the egg white.

2. Refrigerate mixture for 10 minutes, or until it turns cold.

Application:

1. Apply the mixture on your face.

2. Leave it for 15 to 20 minutes.

3. Rinse with warm water, and use cool water as final rinse.

IX. Egg Facial Mask

Many are used to using egg whites for various treatments. But did you know that you can also use the egg yolk as a facial mask? This has a very hydrating effect and also tightens pores.

Ingredient:

1 pc egg

Procedure:

Separate the egg yolk and beat it until smooth.

Application:

1. Apply the beaten egg yolk all over the face.

2. Leave it to dry for 15 minutes.

3. Rinse with lukewarm water.

X. **Egg and Lemon Facial Mask**

Lemon is another ingredient that is favored by many advocates of homemade beauty products. According to some experts, lemon can prove to be harmful for those who have dry skin. However, combining it with other ingredients will remedy that.

Ingredients:

2 eggs

1 tsp lemon juice or lemon extract

1 tsp olive oil

Procedures:

1. Separate egg yolk from egg white. You will only be using the yolk for this recipe.

2. Mix all the ingredients and stir until a paste forms.

Application:

1. Spread the mixture on your clean face.

2. Leave the mixture on for 10 to 15 minutes.

3. Rinse it off using warm water.

XI. Herbal Facial Mask

This mask contains ingredients that have strong cleansing properties, and by adding the egg, it also tightens pores.

Ingredients:

1 tsp dried chamomile flowers, crumbled

1 tsp fresh mint leaves, chopped finely

1 tbsp honey

1 pc egg

Procedures:

1. Place all ingredients in a bowl.

2. Mix until well blended.

Application:

1. Apply mixture on the face and neck, massaging slightly using upward circular motions.

2. Leave the mixture on face and let it dry for 10 to 15 minutes.

3. Rinse face with warm water.

XII. Oatmeal-Honey Facial Mask

On their own, oatmeal and honey are often used in various facial treatments. Mixing them together in a mask makes for a pretty potent combination.

Ingredients:

1/4 cup instant or rolled oats, ground finely

3 tbsp honey

1 tbsp bee pollen

1 tbsp egg, optional (buttermilk or heavy cream are alternatives)

Procedures:

1. Beat egg thoroughly (if you are using egg instead of buttermilk or heavy cream).

2. Combine beaten egg with all the other ingredients and mix until it forms a smooth mixture.

Application:

1. Apply the mixture to clean and dry face.

2. Leave mixture on face and let it dry for 10 to 15 minutes.

3. Rinse off mixture with warm water.

XIII. **Oatmeal-Tomato Facial Mask**

Blemishes may also be cleared off using a combination of oatmeal and tomato.

Ingredients:

1 pc ripe tomato, chopped or diced

1 tbsp instant or rolled oats

1 tsp lemon juice or lemon extract

Procedures:

1. Mix all ingredients in a bowl, or combine them in a blender.

2. Stir or blend until mixture is a paste that may be applied on the face. You may add more oatmeal to make the paste thicker.

Application:

1. Apply the mixture on the face, putting more on areas with spots and blemishes you want removed.

2. Leave the mixture on the face for 10 to 15 minutes.

3. Dip a clean washcloth in warm water and use it to wipe off the mask from your face.

XIV. **Palm Facial Mask**

One of the most dreaded signs of aging is sagging skin. Instead of paying ridiculous amounts of money for procedures to firm up your facial skin, you can make your own firming mask yourself. The good thing about this treatment is that it can also be used on the body, not just the face and the neck.

Ingredients:

1/2 cup heats of palm, chopped

2 pcs bay leaves

1 stalk celery

2 pcs eggs, yolk and white separated

1/4 russet potato, scrubbed, unpeeled

1 tsp mint extract, or 1/4 cup mint leaves, chopped finely

1/2 pc cucumber

1/4 cup wheat germ

1/4 cup powdered milk

1 tsp coconut extract

1 tsp vanilla extract

Procedures:

1. For this recipe, you will only be using egg whites, so separate them cleanly.

2. Combine all ingredients in a blender, and blend at low to medium speed for 45 seconds, or until it turns into a paste.

Application:

1. Apply paste to face as a mask (or the neck and other parts of the body needing firming).

2. Leave on mixture for 15 to 25 minutes.

3. Rinse with warm water.

XV.   **Peppermint Facial Scrub**

Peppermint is ideal for oily skin, so why not add it to your facial scrub and use it for your daily cleansing regimen?

Ingredients:

2 tsp dried peppermint leaves, crumbled

2 tsp dried lavender, crumbled

2 cups rolled oats

1 cup almonds, ground

2 cups white cosmetic clay

Procedures:

1. Mix oats, almonds, peppermint leaves and lavender and grind them using a mortar and pestle. You may also opt to make use of a blender. Grind until they turn powdery.

2. Mix the resulting powder with the cosmetic clay to come up with a patty and store it in a clean, dry container.

Application:

1. Take a chunk of the patty - around 1 teaspoon - and add a little water.

2. Mix the water and mixture until a paste is formed. Be careful not to put too much water; you want a paste, not a runny mixture.

3. Massage the scrub onto your face in circular upward motions.

4. Rinse with warm water.

XVI. **Strawberry and Honey Mask**

Strawberry has been proven as an effective ingredient for body scrubs, but rarely for facial treatments. Those with oily skin will find that strawberries will also be beneficial.

Ingredients:

8 to 10 pcs of medium to large strawberries

3 tbsp honey

Procedures:

1. Mash strawberries or pound them into a pulp, keeping the juice intact. Do not drain.

2. Add honey to the mashed strawberries and mix until it forms into a paste. Do not pound too much or else it will be too watery.

Application:

1. Apply the mixture to the face and leave it on for 10 to 15 minutes.

2. Rinse it off with warm water.

XVII. **Tomato-Lemon Facial Mask**

For those pesky blemishes, you do not have to make use of products that contain bleach, which can potentially harm your skin. With just a piece of tomato and some lemon juice, you can get rid of those blemishes safely.

Ingredients:

1 pc ripe tomato, chopped

1 tsp lemon juice or lemon extract

1 tbsp oatmeal (instant or rolled)

Procedures:

1. Mix chopped tomato, lemon juice and oatmeal in one bowl.

2. You can mix it, stirring vigorously, or use a blender, until a thick paste is formed. If you prefer a thicker facial mask to ensure it stays on the face, you may opt to add more oatmeal.

Application:

1. Spread the mixture on your face, particularly on the areas with blemishes. Let sit for 10 to 15 minutes.

2. Dip a clean washcloth in warm water and use it to wipe face clean of the mixture.

Chapter 4: Homemade Organic Products for the Body

Body scrubs, body lotions, body wash and creams are also considered as essentials when it comes to hygiene and body care. Here are some recipes that you can follow to make your own homemade organic body care products.

I.   Almond-and-Salt Body Scrub

If you do not have almonds readily, an alternative is to use almond oil instead. All you need is to add salt to turn it into a scrub.

Ingredients:

1/4 cup almond oil

1/4 cup almond milk

1/2 cup salt

1.5   oz glycerine soap base

Procedures and application:

Mix all ingredients together. Use as scrub when bathing.

II.　Aloe Vera and Nettle Leaf Soap

Aloe vera is generally good for the skin, so it is highly recommended to include it in a soap recipe.

Ingredients:

2 tsp aloe vera gel

2 tbsp dried nettle leaf, crushed or crumbled

1 cup glycerine soap base

Procedures:

1. Mix all the ingredients over low fire until everything is blended well.

2. Take it out of the fire and let cool for a few minutes.

3. Pour into molds and store in the refrigerator or a cool, dry place, to allow it to set.

III.　Apple Tart Soap

Remember those apple tarts you love to make and eat? This is not the same recipe, but you will definitely love using soap that you made yourself, smelling of apple, and containing safe ingredients.

Ingredients:

4 oz clear glycerine soap, unscented

1 tsp liquid glycerine

1 tbsp liquid soap

1/2 tsp apple fragrance oil

1/2 tsp cinnamon, ground

Procedures:

1. Melt the unscented glycerine soap by placing it in the microwave, or heating it in a pan using low heat.

2. Stir in the liquid glycerine and the liquid soap.

3. Continue stirring while adding the apple fragrance oil and cinnamon.

4. Stir until consistency becomes thick and the cinnamon is evenly distributed.

5. Pour the mixture immediately into molds before they set.

6. Set it aside, or place it in the refrigerator, to allow it time to harden.

IV.   Cinnamon Bar Soap

The exfoliating properties of cinnamon makes it ideal for when one is taking baths and want to remove dead skin.

Ingredients:

1 bar (4 oz) glycerin soap

2 tsp cinnamon powder

8 to 10 drops cinnamon oil

Procedures:

1. Over low fire, melt the soap base.

2. Stir the powdered cinnamon into the liquefied soap.

3. Remove from fire and add the drops of cinnamon oil.

4. Pour into molds and let cool for several hours before using.

V.   Cooling Citrus Body Lotion

Smoothing a soothing lotion, especially one with a citrus scent, will prove to be very energizing. Try this body lotion recipe.

Ingredients:

40 drops orange oil

4 tbsp liquid glycerine

4 tbsp lemon juice or lemon extract

Procedures and application:

1. Combine all ingredients in a clean glass bottle.

2. Cover the bottle tightly and shake until contents are mixed thoroughly.

3. Store in the refrigerator when not in use.

VI. **Creamy Coffee Soap**

Coffee is one of the best antioxidants out there, and when used on your skin, you can be sure that it will also have wonderful effects!

Ingredients:

1 tsp ground espresso (or any roasted coffee beans)

1 bar (4 oz) glycerine soap

1 tsp powdered milk

8 to 10 drops of coffee fragrance oils

Procedures:

1. Melt the glycerin bar soap over low heat.

2. Once it has been fully melted, remove from fire.

3. Stir in ground espresso and powdered milk until well distributed.

4. Add the coffee fragrance oil, depending on how strong you want the coffee scent is.

5. Pour into molds and allow time for it to cool and harden.

VII. **Green Apple and Aloe Vera Shower Gel**

If body scrubs and soaps are not your cup of tea, you could make a shower gel instead.

Ingredients:

2 tbsp aloe vera gel

1/4 cup shampoo concentrate

1/2 tsp table salt or rock salt

3/4 cup distilled water

15 drops apple fragrance oil

1 drop green food coloring (optional)

Procedures:

1. Bring the water to a simmer, but not to a boil.

2. Pour into a ceramic or glass bowl and stir in the shampoo concentrate.

3. Add the aloe vera gel and salt. Mix thoroughly.

4. Stir in the apple fragrance oil and food coloring.

5. Continue stirring until mixture is thick.

6. Pour into a container (or a squeeze bottle, if available).

VIII. **Lavender and Beeswax Soap**

Honey can also be used in your bath and body soap. Just try this recipe, which also adds in lavender to give it a pleasant scent.

Ingredients:

1 tbsp beeswax pellets

1 tbsp honey

1 bar (4 oz) clear glycerine soap

8 to 10 drops lavender oil

Procedures:

1. Melt the beeswax over low fire until it is liquefied. Be sure to keep it warm and in liquid state while you work on the other ingredients.

2. Melt the glycerine soap base in another pan until it has liquefied.

3. Pour the warm and melted beeswax into the soap base and stir to mix.

4. Stir in the honey.

5. Add the lavender oil drops to give it scent.

6. Remove from fire, let cool, and pour into molds. Set aside to let it harden.

IX. **Lavender Milk Cream Liquid Soap and Soak**

The scent of lavender is not the only thing that this shower gel has going on for it. It also contains milk, which is both soothing and moisturizing.

Ingredients:

1 cup powdered milk

3 to 5 drops lavender oil

Procedures and application:

1. Combine the lavender oil and powdered milk and mix them thoroughly.

2. Add the mixture to your running bath water, or as a bath tub soak.

X. **Milk, Honey and Oatmeal Body Scrub**

Milk is good for your skin. Combine that with the moisturizing effect of honey and the exfoliating properties of oatmeal, and you have a winning combination for your body scrub!

Ingredients:

2 tbsp whole milk powder

2 tbsp oatmeal, instant or rolled

2 tbsp powdered honey

2 capsules Vitamin E

1/2 tsp vanilla powder (optional)

Procedures and application:

1. Use a coffee grinder (or something similar) to grind oatmeal finely.

2. Add contents of the vitamin E capsules and grind again.

3. Add whole milk powder and powdered honey and grind for another 10 seconds.

4. In a separate bowl, put mixture and add warm water sparingly while mixing, until it forms a paste.

5. Add the vanilla powder for a refreshing and natural scent.

6. Use paste as a scrub.

XI.   **Orange Peel and Oats Scrub**

Citrus fruits have always been known to be good for the skin, which is why you have seen lemon juice and lemon extract mentioned many times over in many homemade organic beauty products recipes. This time, we will make use of orange. However, we're not using the juicy part. Instead, we will use its peel.

Ingredients:

1 cup dried orange peels

1 cup oatmeal, cooked

1 cup almonds

Procedures and application:

1. Place the orange peels, cooked oats and almonds in a food processor and process until it turns powdery. You can make it easier and faster by using pre-ground almonds.

2. Add several drops of water to the powder, just enough to moisten it, and use as body scrub.

XII.   **Orange Poppy Body Scrub**

Poppy seeds also provide exfoliating action and, combined with the rejuvenating effects of orange, you have a refreshing body scrub with a citrusy scent that you will definitely enjoy.

Ingredients:

1/4 tsp orange essential oil

1/2 cup poppy seeds

1/2 cup olive oil

Procedures and application:

Combine all the ingredients together and store in a bottle. One tablespoon should be enough to be used each time. Massage the scrub gently against your skin when you bathe.

XIII. **Peaches and Cream Soap**

Many are aspiring to have a peaches-and-cream complexion. To do that, you have to focus on caring for your skin. How about a peaches and cream soap to make that happen?

Ingredients:

1 bar Castile soap, shredded

1/4 cup powdered milk

1/4 cup distilled water

1 tbsp sweet almond oil

8 to 10 drops peach fragrance oil

Procedures:

1. In a saucepan, pour the distilled water and let simmer over low heat.

2. Add the shredded soap and stir until it turns into a sticky mass.

3. Remove from heat.

4. Stir in the powdered milk, sweet almond oil and peach fragrance oil. Mix until fully blended.

5. Pour in molds and set aside to let it cool and harden.

XIV. **Peach Shower Gel**

Stay moisturized from head to toe with this peach shower gel, which also contains vitamin E essence.

Ingredients:

1/4 cup shampoo concentrate

1 tsp table salt

3/4 cup distilled water

15 drops of peach fragrance oil

2 capsules Vitamin E (containing 5-6 drops of vitamin E oil)

1 tbsp apricot kernel oil

Procedures:

1. Bring the water into a simmer, but not to a boil.

2. Add the salt and apricot kernel oil, followed by the peach fragrance oil and the vitamin E oil.

3. Keep stirring until mixture becomes thick.

4. Pour into a container, or a squeeze bottle.

XV. **Peppermint Lotion**

If you have problem with itchy skin, applying this peppermint lotion will easily solve that.

Ingredients:

3 to 4 drops peppermint oil

1/2 cup rubbing alcohol

1/2 cup distilled water

Procedures and application:

1. Pour distilled water into a bottle, followed by the rubbing alcohol.

2. Add the peppermint oil.

3. Close the cap of the bottle tightly and shake well until ingredients are mixed together.

4. Apply to skin using cotton balls or a clean piece of cloth.

XVI. **Scented Body Salts**

Salt also acts as an excellent exfoliating agent, so we will make use of that in this body scrub recipe.

Ingredients:

1 cup salt (fine or rock salt will do, but it will be best to mix them up for varying texture)

1 cup olive oil (vegetable oil and canola oil are alternatives)

1 cup liquid soap, unscented

3 to 5 drops of any mildly scented oil (your preference)

Procedures and application:

Mix all the ingredients in one bowl until well-blended. Use the mixture as a scrub, gently massaging it on your skin when you bathe.

XVII. **Sugar Body Scrub**

Salt is not the only condiment from your kitchen that you can use as a body scrub. Sugar is also another excellent ingredient.

Ingredients:

2 cups granulated sugar

1/2 cup canola oil (or olive oil)

Procedures and application:

Combine granulated sugar and canola oil in a bowl and mix thoroughly. Since sugar melts easily, you must use it immediately after mixing together so you can still take advantage of its exfoliating action before it melts.

XVIII. **Sweet Scrub**

Here is a very simple recipe that once again utilizes sugar and its exfoliating actions.

Ingredients:

3 tsp plain yogurt, unsweetened and unflavored

1 tbsp granulated sugar

1 tsp brewer's yeast

Procedures and application:

Mix all three ingredients together until a paste is formed. Use as a scrub. However, just like the Sugar Body Scrub, you must use it immediately instead of storing it.

Chapter 5: Homemade Organic Products for the Hair

Your hair is your crowning glory, so it makes sense that you also give it a lot of care and attention. Shampoos, conditioners and hair treatment products may also be made using various ingredients that you can easily score.

I.   Avocado Hair Conditioner

For that nourished and healthy hair, you may use avocado and mayonnaise as hair conditioner.

Ingredients:

1/2 pc avocado

1 small jar of mayonnaise

Procedures and application:

1. Put the two ingredients in a bowl. Make sure the avocado has been peeled.

2. Mash them together, mixing them thoroughly.

3. Take the mixture and smooth onto hair, from the scalp down to the tips.

4. Wrap hair in a shower cap (cling wrap or Saran wrap will also do the trick).

5. Let the conditioner do its thing for 15 to 20 minutes. Rinse after.

II.   Chamomile Shampoo

More than just a calming ingredient usually found in teas, chamomile may also be used in your shampoo.

Ingredients:

1 cup of fresh chamomile flowers (or 4 small teabags of chamomile tea)

4 tbsp clear, unscented glycerine soap, shredded or flaked

3 tsp liquid glycerine

Procedures and application:

1. Boil 1 ½ cups of water in a saucepan or small kettle.

2. Upon boiling, steep the chamomile teabags the water for 10 minutes.

3. Remove the teabags and add the soap flakes or shredded soap into the remaining water.

4. Leave the soap flakes in the water until they soften and turn into a sticky mass.

5. Stir in liquid glycerine and mix thoroughly until the mixture thickens.

6. Store in a container and let cool before using as shampoo.

III. Coconut Shampoo

Coconut is a popular ingredient when it comes to shampoos, and you can also make your own coconut shampoo by following this recipe. Make sure you have a thermometer with you!

Ingredients:

1 lb (7 oz) coconut oil

2 lb (10 oz) olive oil

1 lb (7 oz) vegetable shortening, solid-type

2 lb (10 oz) lye

2 oz liquid glycerin

2 oz castor oil

1/2 oz alcohol

2 pints cold distilled water

Procedures:

1. Place a wide-mouthed container in a large pan.

2. Mix all the oils together (except the castor oil) in the wide-mouthed container. Set aside oil mixture.

3. In another container, mix 2 pints of cold water and lye. Stir until the lye solution has cooled.

4. Pour lye solution in a glass container and place in another large pan.

5. Simultaneously heat up the two pans (with the oil mixture and the lye solution) by pouring hot water on the pan, outside the containers. Bring them both between 95 to 98 degrees Fahrenheit.

6. Add the lye solution to the oil mixture, stirring continuously. The color will become opaque, then brown. Don't worry; that is normal. The color will lighten afterwards.

7. It is ready when it has a similar consistency with sour cream. When it

is ready, add the glycerin, alcohol and castor oil. Stir until fully mixed.

8. Store in a squeeze bottle.

IV.   Egg Shampoo

It's not just your skin, but also your hair, that will benefit from eggs.

Ingredients:

1 pc egg

1 tbsp mild unscented shampoo (or Castile soap)

1 tsp olive oil

8 drops lavender oil (optional)

Procedures and application:

1. Place all ingredients in a blender and blend until smooth.

2. Since egg is the main ingredient, use it as a shampoo immediately. If there are any left over, store it in the refrigerator, but no more than a day.

V.   Honey and Egg Shampoo

This shampoo is very easy to prepare, and also happens to contain two ingredients that are good for locking in moisture in your hair.

Ingredients:

1 pc egg, large size

1/4 cup raw honey

2 tbsp liquid soap

1 tbsp witch hazel

1 tbsp almond oil or wheat germ oil

2 tbsp water

1 tbsp rosewater or lavender oil (optional)

Procedures and application:

1. Combine all ingredients, except egg, in a wide-mouthed, screw-top jar.

2. In a separate bowl, beat egg until fluff and smooth.

3. Pour beaten egg into the earlier mixture.

4. Close the lid tightly and shake well until the mixture is well-blended.

5. Use as you would normal shampoo.

VI. Honey and Herbs Hair Conditioner

Honey may also be used for deep conditioning of the hair.

Ingredients:

1/4 cup raw honey

1/4 cup liquid glycerine

1/4 cup dried sage leaves, crumbled

1/2 cup dried chamomile flowers, crumbled

1/2 cup witch hazel

Procedures and application:

1. Combine all the ingredients in a jar. Close the lid of the jar tightly.

2. Shake the jar until all ingredients have been thoroughly mixed.

3. Set aside for 1 hour.

4. Remove the herbs by using a strainer. You will be left with only the liquid portion.

5. Apply as hair conditioner, letting it remain in your hair for up to 5 minutes before rinsing.

VII.   Honey and Pollen Shampoo

1/4 cup honey

2 tbsp bee pollen

1/2 cup liquid glycerine

1 tbsp witch hazel

1 tsp liquid soap

1 tbsp alcohol

1/4 cup orange flower water (or rosewater)

Procedures and application:

1. Combine all ingredients in a wide-mouthed, screw-top jar.

2. Close the lid tightly and shake well until the mixture is well-blended.

3. Use as you would any shampoo.

VIII. Honey Hair Treatment

Sometimes, you do not need more than two ingredients to come up with a treatment for very dry and damaged hair.

Ingredients:

3 tbsp raw honey

1 tbsp olive oil

Procedures and application:

1. In a small bowl, mix the two ingredients together until the mixture is smooth.

2. After shampooing, apply the mixture to hair, especially to the dry tips.

3. Let it set for 10 to 15 minutes before rinsing with warm water.

IX. Milk and Honey Hair Conditioner

If you have extra buttermilk powder lying around the house, you already have the first ingredient for a deep conditioning homemade hair treatment.

Ingredients:

2 tbsp buttermilk powder

1/4 cup liquid glycerine

1/3 cup hot water

2 tbsp liquid lecithin

1/4 cup raw honey

1/4 cup dried sage leaves, crumbled

Procedures and application:

1. Put sage leaves on the hot water and let steep for 10 minutes.

2. Strain the water to remove the sage leaves.

3. Stir in all the other ingredients into the herbal water, until everything is mixed thoroughly.

4. Apply to hair after shampooing, leaving it on for 3 minutes before rinsing.

X.   Mint Herbal Shampoo

For a refreshing shampoo that will soothe your scalp, mint is always one of your best bets.

Ingredients:

2 tbsp dry peppermint leaves, crumbled

2 tbsp dry spearmint leaves, crumbled

1 tbsp dry safe leaves, crumbled

2/3 cup baby shampoo (or any mild shampoo)

1 cup distilled water

Procedures:

1. In a saucepan, combine water, peppermint, spearmint, and sage, until the water boils.

2. When the water has boiled, remove from heat and let steep for 20 to 25 minutes. This will also give it time to cool.

3. Strain the herbs from the water.

4. Combine the baby shampoo with the water, and mix thoroughly.

5. Pour the mixture in a squeeze bottle.

Chapter 6: Other Homemade Organic Products

If you take the plunge and decide to start making your beauty products and treatments at home, you will come to realize that the possibilities are endless! In fact, you can even go without the commercially sold and manufactured products being sold in the market altogether! Here are other recipes that you should try out.

I.   **Apple-Pear Night Cream**

Night creams are becoming increasingly popular because they are designed to lessen wrinkles. With the choices ingredients, you can definitely come up with an anti-wrinkle night cream that is even more effective than those expensive commercial brands.

Ingredients:

1 tsp apple juice or extract

1/4 pc pear

2 egg whites

1 tsp lemon juice

1 tsp lime juice

3 pcs seedless grapes

2 tbsp buttermilk powder

1 tbsp rosemary leaves, dried and crumbled

Procedures and application:

1. Put all ingredients in a blender and whiff for 30 seconds. The setting should be at medium speed.

2. Pour the blended mixture in a small jar with a cover.

3. Use a cotton ball to dip into the mixture, and slowly dab around the eye area, and other parts of the face where wrinkles are visible.

4. Let mixture dry, and rinse with warm water.

5. Pat your face dry with a clean towel and apply moisturizer.

6. Use the night cream 3 times a week only.

7. Prepare sparingly, as the mixture will only be effective for a period of 4 days.

II. Avocado Eye Cream

The areas around the eyes are especially sensitive, so it is not advisable to apply just any drugstore product around it. To be on the safe side, make your own eye cream instead.

Ingredients:

3 slices of ripe avocado

5 drops almond oil

Procedure and application:

1. Mix avocado and almond oil in a blender. Blend until thoroughly mixed.

2. Use a cotton ball to dab the mixture around the eyes.

3. Leave for 5 minutes and rinse with warm water.

III. Beach Sand and Canola Foot Scrub

Caring for your feet is also very important, especially if the nature of your work entails standing all day or moving constantly. Remember those times when you step on the beach and unconsciously dig your feet and toes into the sand, loving the relaxing feeling the sand gives you? You can actually make use of beach sand in making your own foot scrub. It is relaxing and also exfoliates your feet at the same time.

Ingredients:

2 tbsp beach sand

2 tbsp canola oil

3 to 5 drops of rosemary oil

Procedures and application:

1. Combine all ingredients and mix into a scrub.

2. Massage the beach sand and canola oil foot scrub onto your feet, focusing on the most problematic areas.

IV. **Beeswax and Coconut Hand Cream**

Your hands are two of the most abused parts of your body, so it deserves just as much care as you give the rest of your body.

Ingredients:

1/4 cup beeswax

1/4 cup coconut oil

3 tbsp baby oil (or even olive oil)

1/3 cup liquid glycerine

Procedures and application:

1. In a small saucepan or over a double boiler, melt the beeswax, mixing coconut oil as you do.

2. Once the beeswax is melted and thoroughly mixed with the coconut oil, add the rest of the ingredients, stirring constantly for about 5 minutes.

3. Pour the mixture into a glass container while it is still hot.

4. Use as hand cream.

V. **Beeswax Lip Balm**

Want beestung lips? What about trying out this beeswax lip balm?

Ingredients:

2 tbsp beeswax

1 tbsp coconut oil

Procedures:

1. Using a saucepan over a stove, or a double boiler, melt the beeswax, while slowly adding in the coconut oil.

2. While it is still hot, pour melted mixture into a glass container. Let it harden.

3. Use directly on the lips as a soothing and moisturizing balm.

VI.   **Chocolate Lip Gloss**

Add a bit of gloss, with a yummy chocolate-y taste, to your lips with this recipe!

Ingredients:

2 tbsp cocoa butter, grated

1 tsp coconut oil

2 pcs vitamin E capsules

1/4 tsp chocolate, grated into chips

Procedures:

1. In a double boiler, melt the cocoa butter, adding in the coconut oil and the vitamin E oil contained in the capsules. You may also use the microwave to melt them altogether.

2. Stir in the grated chocolate chips until everything is melted.

3. Pour the mixture into a glass container while still hot. Let it harden and cool before using.

VII. **Cocoa Butter Hand Cream**

You will find a lot of cocoa butter creams being sold in the market, but why buy when you can make your own?

Ingredients:

4 tbsp cocoa butter

4 tbsp beeswax

4 tbsp almond oil

Procedures and application:

1. Melt the cocoa butter and the beeswax together, stirring constantly to avoid clumping.

2. Stir in the almond oil and continue stirring until the mixture is smooth.

3. Pour the mixture in a squeeze bottle or a glass jar.

4. Set aside and let it harden before using it as hand cream.

VIII. Cucumber Wrinkle Cream

Instead of just placing slices of cucumber over your eyes, you can maximize its wonderful effects by creating your own anti-wrinkle cream, using cucumber as the main ingredient.

Ingredients:

1/2 pc cucumber

1 pc egg

2 tbsp mayonnaise

1/2 cup olive oil (avocado oil or wheat germ are also good alternatives)

IX. Euphoric Bath Salts

There are a lot of products being sold that make use of sea salts as their main component. You, too, can make your own sea salt-based bath products!

Ingredients:

3 tbsp sea salt

2 tbsp Epsom salt

3 tbsp baking soda

8 to 10 drops of any essential oil

Choices of oil include Apricot Kernel, Avocado Oil, Bergamot, Chamomile, Cinnamon Oil, Grapefruit, Jasmine, Lavender, Orange, Peach, Pine Balsam, Rose, Rosewood, Sandalwood, Vanilla, Ylang Ylang.

Procedures and application:

1. Mix all ingredients in a tightly lidded jar. (A Ziploc bag will also work, just make sure to seal it tightly before proceeding to the next step.)

2. Close the lid and gently shake to mix the contents very well.

3. Add to the bath tub in running water, or you may also mix it in as a soak.

X.   **Herbal Toothpaste**

You'll be surprised at how easy it is to make your own toothpaste.

Ingredients:

1/4 tsp spearmint oil

1/4 tsp peppermint oil

1/4 cup arrowroot

1 tsp sage, ground

1/4 cup powdered orrisroot

1/4 cup distilled water

Procedures:

1. Combine all the dry ingredients in a bowl.

2. Start adding in the water while stirring, eventually forming a paste. Continue stirring until it achieves the consistency you want for a toothpaste.

3. Pour mixture in a jar and cover it tightly. Store at room temperature.

Conclusion

Thank you again for downloading this book!

I hope this book was able to help you to come up with your own hair, facial and body care products using the choicest of natural and organic ingredients. Granted, this book contains only a few homemade beauty recipes. There are still a lot of recipes out there that you can follow. In fact, if you are adventurous enough and you want to experiment, you can even come up with your own recipes!

Whether you are making them for yourself or you want to give them away to family and friends as presents, you will definitely have the guarantee that these products are safe and effective, and they also have something that other commercial products don't have: your personal touch.

66

Now you have been armed with the recipes. The next step is to look for the best ingredients and start making these homemade organic beauty care products. Stay natural, stay beautiful! Stay naturally beautiful with these wonderful products that you made yourself!

Thank you and good luck!

WaraWaran Roongruangsri

You can be gorgeous at thirty, charming at forty,

and irresistible for the rest of your life.

- Coco Chanel

Printed in Great Britain
by Amazon